New Paradigms

By

Tom Reidy

Dedicated To

Al Matthews

(1934-2005)

One of my Air Force cronies who always thought outside of the box.

Preface

New Paradigms is not revolutionary thinking. It is simply common sense principles applied to some areas of the public forum that need change and reform. It never ceases to amaze me how we complicate so many aspects of our individual lives as well as the political, economic, and social arenas. It's really true that all problems have simple solutions but human nature seems to have a deeply embedded desire to complicate everything.

I said *simple* solutions -- not always easy -- but *simple*. So why don't we just implement them? I don't know, but I do know that these paradigms I present in this book will probably never see daylight. Political Correctness, bureaucracy, and the old "We can't do that because…" mentality will always prevail. This compulsion to complexity is one of the factors that is ruining our country and our way of life.

I present detailed outlines for reforming welfare, the penal system, jury reform, presidential campaigns, state and local government reform, economic reforms, immigration reform, and Social Security and Medicare reforms.   They would need tweaking and perfecting but the outline and structure is based on sound thinking.

Let the reader be the final judge of their worth.

Tom Reidy
Sep. 30, 2015
Tacoma, WA

Table of Contents

Nine REALLY Simple Ways To Make Government More Efficient

This paradigm pertains only to the Federal Government. The Constitution calls for "sovereign states" because each state has different needs and operates under different sets of circumstances so each state needs to establish policies that meet its specific needs. This brings us to sub-paradigm Number One.

Stop *subsidizing state governments to support their programs.*

Billions and billions of federal dollars go to subsidize state governments mostly to support their social programs. California (among several others) is surviving on Federal Life Support. Until recent decades, the Feds sent very little money to individual states. Today, most states could not survive without Federal dollars. It is imperative that we end this dependency. It cannot be done overnight. States will have to be weaned off the Feds. It will take years to phase out this dependency but we need to arrive at a time when Federal money to the states would be in the form of loans repayable with interest. (The only exception would be disaster relief.)   This would take a huge burden off the federal budget. I mentioned California as the prime example of Federal dependency. During the current economic crisis (2011) the Feds are GIVING California millions of dollars to pay the state's unemployment benefits.

End ALL federal subsidies.

Why are we subsidizing farmers, the oil companies, or anyone else for that matter? The tax system I outline below would eliminate any excuse or "justification" for subsidies.

Make Social Security a Public Trust under private sector management.

This smacks of privatization, which it is, and we remember the furor Liberals raised in 2005 when President George W. Bush wanted to allow people to be able to invest a whopping 2 percent of their Social Security contributions in private sector investments. We will discuss this below in the paradigm on Social Security Reform.

Reward government agencies for saving money.

Stop the frantic spend downs that government agencies feel compelled to do toward the end of every fiscal year. The idea is that if we don't spend, spend, spend they will think we don't need it and give us a smaller budget next year. Instead REWARD the agency and its staff with a financial bonus for being wise stewards of their budgets. This spend down mentality contributes to hundreds of millions -- if not billions -- of dollars in waste every year.

Make Amtrak and the United States Postal Service profit making operations or sell them.

There is nothing wrong with the Federal Government -- or state governments -- making a profit. Port Authorities turn a profit and governments charge fees for all kinds of services. Amtrak and the Post Office have been losing billions of dollars for years because they are under *government management* -- an oxymoron if there ever was one. Put them under the supervision of professional private sector managers with proven track records of profit making and innovative management and they will likely make money -- a lot of money. If they don't, sell them. Even if a foreign company purchases them they will still be paying taxes to the U.S. Government. The reason why these entities are money losers is because bureaucrats who do not manage with innovation run them and Congress, another inefficient entity, gets involved. They do not understand business principles and are terrified of thinking outside the box. Their only solution is more regulation and raising prices.

Sell off government lands at Fair Market Value.

There are millions of acres of government land that are just sitting there. They could be bringing in billions of dollars in revenue. If the land has oil or other commodities, lease them and share the profits. This means that we would have to lift some of the environmental regulations but we need to become self-sufficient in energy so this is a win-win proposition. Of course, in today's political climate this will not happen.

Review all federal departments and agencies not specifically required by the Constitution or National Security needs.

The Department of Education is a prime example of this. President Jimmy Carter created it as a sop to the Teachers' Unions. According to a report on *The O'Reilly Factor* a few years ago, this Department has wasted billions and cannot account for millions. The Department of Energy could be justified since energy resources are a national security issue. Before making a decision to outright abolish a department or agency, review all of its functions to determine if it has a valid purpose or could be incorporated into another department or agency. ALL Federal departments and agencies should undergo desk level audits to weed out unnecessary, redundant, and duplicated tasks. There should be no overlapping of work between different departments and agencies. Simplify complex reporting functions.

The key word to all of this is *simplify*.

Review EVERY SINGLE Federal regulation and eliminate those that create unnecessary paperwork and unnecessarily restrict businesses and simplify the rest.

Excessive regulation has severely restricted the growth of small business. When small businesses can't hire and/or have to lay off, unemployment goes up. Excessive regulation costs businesses an estimated $300 billion annually. It is a major cause of outsourcing by larger companies.

9. *Simplify the Federal Taxation System.*

It is too complex and has too many loopholes. It is a political football used by both parties: the Republicans use it as a carrot to attract voters with promises to cut taxes while the Democrats as a stick to provoke class envy by promising to "soak the rich."

Here is the solution and what it would accomplish A flat corporate tax of 15 percent and a flat personal income tax of 10 percent for everyone making over $50.000,00. Those making less than 50K would not be required to pay any Federal Income Tax although they may be required to pay state income tax and a Federal exemption would help offset the state tax requirement. The Earned Income Tax Credit would be abolished. We cannot afford it with an $18 trillion National Debt. In addition, there would be a two percent Federal Sales Tax that everyone would pay. The Capital Gains tax rate would be 10 percent.

The Simplified Tax would level the playing field.
There would be no loopholes, no deductions, and no exemptions would be allowed except for medicine and medical expenses not covered by insurance.
It would reduce housing prices.

Homebuyers are willing to commit to outrageous mortgages because they are "deductible." Eliminating the mortgage deductible would eliminate a lot of that willingness.
It would stimulate the economy.

The Capital Gains Tax would be 10 percent making the United States an attractive place for foreign investment.
It would be a pay as you go system.

For employees, the tax would be deducted from each paycheck taking some of the pain out of it. Corporations, the self-employed and private contractors etc. would pay quarterly. Businesses and corporations collecting the Federal Sales Tax would pay this tax quarterly as well. Capital Gains taxes would be deducted by the brokerage firm or account manager at the time of sale.

   It would greatly reduce the size, scope, and power of the Internal Revenue Service

  The Simplified Tax could pay down the National Debt and eradicate deficits.

  It would greatly reduce tax evasion and fraud.

 Congress could pass a Balanced Budget Amendment.

   Will these nine concepts ever be implemented in the present political climate?
NOT A SNOWBALL'S CHANCE IN HELL!!!

Kibbutz 'em

(Based on an Idea by two of my co-workers Judy Sennett and Craig Detmer.)

Under the Welfare Reform Act of 1996, welfare recipients are subject to a lifetime limit of 60 months cash assistance. Those receiving cash assistance are on the Temporary Assistance to Needy Families program (TANF) that replaced Aid to Families with Dependent Children (AFDC). The 60-month time limit does not include food stamps, medical care, and other forms of public assistance such as subsidized daycare and Section 8 (public) housing -- only cash assistance.

So why isn't Welfare Reform working as it was designed to? The majority of TANF recipients are single mothers. The rest are married and unmarried couples with children. Most of these folks are on public assistance because they lack basic life skills. They lack high school diplomas or GEDs and driver's licenses. They have substance abuse and domestic violence issues, are homeless, couch surfing at friends' homes, living in shelters, or are facing eviction. A single mom with little education and work experience and three or four children relying on public transportation to get her kids to daycare and then pound the pavement looking for a fast food job is too bogged down in survival logistics to hold a job. Many Welfare recipients get jobs and lose them within days, weeks, or months since they cannot cope with the survival logistics and are right back on the system. Most of the jobs they get do not pay enough to support a family. They are still dependent on various other forms of Public Assistance (Food Stamps. Medicaid, subsidized daycare) beyond their cash grant. Their cash grant is wiped out because even a minimum wage job far exceeds their grant amount. There are supportive services -- clothing allowance, car repairs, diaper vouchers etc. but these are inadequate to meet most needs. State Welfare agencies dump recipients into job search without properly addressing barriers.

Welfare recipients are being set up to fail and fail they do. The system doesn't care because if a welfare recipient goes to work for one day, the office they are attached to gets a "ticky mark" making the program look good. "Look at all the people we're putting to work," the Governor proclaims as he or she points to the statistics. These statistics include the 9th grade drop out that gets a job at the County Fair for three weeks. She will only work for three weeks at minimum wage but the ticky mark is the same as if she got a $100,000.00 per year job at Microsoft.

Many Welfare recipients are living in unstable and substandard conditions. They are often one step ahead of eviction and utilities shutoff or their rattle trap cars are running on rubber bands. Support services are insufficient and they are back on the public assistance merry-go-round sometimes before they come off the local office database. The majority lack the skills and education to hold anything beyond minimum wage jobs. Training programs have proved a failure because they are not successful at placing graduates in jobs. They flood the market with more graduates than the labor market needs. These programs do not always provide the experience employers require.

We are dealing with a culture of Generational Poverty that does not subscribe to middle class standards and will adapt to the system no matter how much hassle we build into it for them. And we do build in hassle -- dress codes, daily attendance requirements, mandatory classes, and more-- but this "aversion therapy" has proven fruitless. Many Welfare recipients are "system people" and they know how to navigate and manipulate it.

It's time to admit that Welfare Reform has not lived up to expectations. Replace it with the Kibbutz system. Anyone seeking Welfare cash assistance would be required to live in a state-sponsored Kibbutz. Here are the advantages:

It would eliminate homelessness and evictions.

The Kibbutz would be an option for the homeless with or without children as well as people receiving TANF. It would eliminate one of the greatest pressures of being poor -- the lack of stable housing, frequent moves and evictions, periods of homelessness, and going from one roach infested drug drop apartment complex to another. A stable environment would go a long way in eliminating some of the conditions that keep people on Public Assistance.

All basic needs would be met.

Food, personal hygiene items, and health care would be available on site. Newly minted doctors, dentists, optometrist's etc. could pay off their student loans by working for two or three years in a Kibbutz. Only major medical emergencies that required hospitalization would be handled off site.

Residents would provide daycare at the kibbutz.

Affordable, safe, and dependable daycare is another major obstacle for single mothers obtaining and keeping employment. The kibbutz would offer on site daycare staffed and run by kibbutz residents.

The Kibbutz would develop its own businesses and eventually become privately owned and managed by the residents.

Residents would share in the earnings and profits as long as they remained in the Kibbutz. The kibbutzes would remain under government oversight but government could partner with faith-based organizations to help set up and manage the kibbutz system.

There would be no time limit.

People could live in the kibbutz for as long as they wished. Anyone working an outside job would be required to pay a part of their salaries to the kibbutz at a rate proportional to their wages. They would still be required to perform some work at the kibbutz and would share in the earnings and profits of the kibbutz business.

Every kibbutz resident would be required to work.

Those who are physically able to work will work or they will be expelled from the kibbutz. The kibbutz would instill structure, discipline, and a work ethic into members' lives. Too many people are on Welfare because they lack these virtues. Those who refused to work would find themselves on the street while their children remained in the custody and care of the kibbutz.

It would eliminate the need for foster care.

The foster care program has been another mega-disaster. Some foster homes are good but too many run the gamut from indifferent to substandard or abusive. . Some foster parents are caring but others are in it for the money and the children pay the price.

Drugs and alcohol would be prohibited on the kibbutz premises.

Anyone bringing in drugs would find themselves in jail and barred from the kibbutz until they had completed a mandatory treatment program. Random drug testing could be required for all kibbutz residents..

Domestic violence would be reduced considerably.

It would be difficult to conceal in the kibbutz environment.

The kibbutz system would could replace the culture of Generational Poverty by providing a stable and structured community environment.

I would like to see a requirement that unmarried couples get married as a pre-requisite for entering the kibbutz. Children follow their parents' example as they grow up seeing mom or dad sleeping with multiple partners. The kibbutz cannot be an ersatz whorehouse.

The savings in TANF cash grants, food stamps, subsidized daycare, emergency rent and utility assistance, Medicaid, foster care, and supportive services would be enormous.

All of these services would be "built in" under one roof.

I was originally against this idea when it was first floated by some of my co-workers. "These people would kill each other in that kind of arrangement," I said. And there would be resistance at first but when the other option is the street there wouldn't be a choice. Remember, there will be no cash grant for rent or utilities, no food stamps or medical insurance for the kibbutz eligible. People would be matched according to their personalities and interests. It would take some adjustment and the startup would no doubt be difficult and meet with resistance but, if successful, would be a vast improvement over the present system.

As a citizen and taxpayer I have heard quite enough of rights and entitlements. I want to hear about responsibilities and earnings. A kibbutz culture could go a long way toward replacing the Generational Poverty culture that has contributed to a decline in national productivity and a rise in crime and out-of-wedlock births.

This is NOT Communism, which is nothing more than an atheistic, social, and economic malfunction. The kibbutz has its basis in Scripture. The early Christians lived this kind of lifestyle as described in the Book of Acts.

All Time Is Hard Time

(Based on an idea by Richard Kain and the author)

Corrections (a euphemism if there ever was one) cost federal, state and local governments a disproportionately high percentage of tax revenues. Prisons do not rehabilitate; the recidivism rate proves that. Gangs and drug dealers run prisons. In some prisons, correctional officers have little or no control. Walla Walla State Penitentiary in Washington State in the 1970s was the sole proprietorship of inmate motorcycle gang members. Lifers in California's Pelican Island Correctional Facility run their outside criminal operations from behind bars. In nearly all prisons, homosexual rape is epidemic. Younger, vulnerable, and non-violent prisoners have a free market value in prison equivalent to the price of a pack of cigarettes. Bubba trades them like commodities. Prisons become battlefields as White, Black, and Latino gangs fight for prison turf. Prison authorities are, to a large extent, powerless in their efforts to maintain control due to the exaggerated set of rights granted to prisoners that will not allow prison authorities to crack down as they should. A prisoner in Washington State in the 1990s stuffed himself full of junk food and ballooned up to 400 pounds so the State could not hang him since, at that weight, he would slowly strangle on the noose constituting "cruel and unusual" punishment.

Everyone agrees the prison system needs reform. Unfortunately, what I am about to propose here is impossible under the current political and social climate that ties the hands of authorities to punish -- and that's what prison should be all about: *punishment*.

We begin by separating the violent from the non-violent. (Non-violent drug offenders should be put into forced rehabilitation.) Most of these people are not "criminals" but need to be purged of their habit. This leaves violent offenders -- members of criminal gangs, sexual predators of all stripes, murderers, rapists, armed robbers, kidnappers, drug dealers, spouse and child abusers, as well as burglars since they are potentially dangerous if cornered and are often prepared to inflict harm if confronted. These people need to be **PUNISHED** for the damage they have caused to people's lives -- much of it irreversible -- and they must be punished in such a way that it will present a serious and credible deterrent to others.

(AUTHOR'S NOTE: Membership in violent gangs -- drug gangs like the Crips and Bloods, MS-13, and such organizations should be a federal offense and vigorously prosecuted and *punished*.)

The new prison paradigm would have two main structures:

Strict Regime Labor Camps

All violent crimes against persons and property would *be **federal*** offenses.

Housing would be in makeshift barracks or tents in remote locations. (Alaska and the Aleutian Islands would be excellent locations if work could be transported to them.) Each prisoner would have his/her own cubicle with walls going three-fourths of the way to the ceiling. Prisoners would be chained to the wall of the cubicle or a stake on the floor allowing just enough mobility to move around the space of the "cube." A shotgun guard will patrol each "cube" row and each cube will be equipped with a surveillance camera.

Each convict will be responsible for cleaning his or her own cubicle. This should be no problem since the cube will consist only of a cot, a latrine bucket, and a wash tub.

Communication between convicts would be strictly forbidden. This would prevent the formation of gangs. **(AUTHOR'S NOTE: Certain orders of religious monks and nuns observe perpetual silence. If they can do it, so can convicts.)**

Toilet facilities would consist of a bucket in each cubicle that would be collected, emptied, and sterilized by convict labor every morning.

Meals will be Army style Meals-Read -To-Eat (MREs). Each convict will receive three each day along with one daily mega-vitamin supplement. Beverages will be limited to water and fruit juices; no coffee and, of course, no alcohol.

Convicts will work six days a week. The only holiday observed will be Christmas. The work day will begin at 7 A.M. and end at 5 P.M. with two fifteen minute breaks in the morning, a thirty minute lunch at noon and two fifteen minute breaks in the afternoon. All work will be hard physical labor. Convict labor could be used to construct and maintain state and national parks and roads or be rented out to agricultural businesses to bring in crops if these businesses could not find sufficient legal labor. Farmers and agribusiness would pay for this service and help defer the cost of maintaining the labor camps. Convict labor could be used to clean up hazardous waste sites. Such assignments would require mobility so quarters could be tents or modular barracks suitable for quick set-ups and dismantling. Convicts will be shackled at all times during the workday.

Convicts will shower twice a week in fall and winter and three times a week during spring and summer.

Sunday is a rest day. Religious services and chaplains will be available that day. On Sunday prison barbers will shave the heads of male and female inmates and the faces of male convicts. No convict will be allowed a personal razor.

Convicts who break any camp regulation (e.g., silence) will be assigned to a pile of boulders, issued a sledge hammer and will spend the work day reducing it to a pile of pebbles no matter how long it takes.

Each labor camp will have an infirmary and prisoners will receive adequate medical care.

Labor camp prisoners will not be allowed visitors and correspondence will be limited to immediate family members once a month.

Convicts will not have access to radio, television, the Internet, or printed material except for a Bible. Non-Christian convicts will be allowed their religious books.

With prison conditions such as these, the death penalty will be unnecessary.   Life sentences would be mandatory for crimes including pre-meditated first degree murder, some rape cases, sex offenses against minors under the age of 15, and the more dangerous criminal gang members. Since violent crime will be a federal offense all sentences will be standardized. No sentence will be less than ten years.

Work and House Arrest

The focus on white-collar criminals needs to be on restitution. House arrest, community service, ankle bracelets, and any combination thereof would be more effective than keeping these people in taxpayer funded jails. Those guilty of financial malfeasance should be forced to pay back as much as possible. For example, instead of incarcerating Bernie Madoff, sell off all his property leaving him enough to live in a small apartment chained to an ankle bracelet and make him work at odd jobs taking everything after he has met his basic monthly expenses. He would be restricted to this (very) small studio apartment when not working. These prisoners would be allowed a track phone for emergencies but no other electronic equipment. Their phone would be strictly monitored. They would be eligible for family visits. One escape attempt would land the offender in a strict regime camp.

Let the punishment fit the crime; hard time for violent criminals and restitution based penalties for non-violent financial criminals.

Certain types of offenders need to be adjudicated on a case-by-case basis. Low level assault, certain types of drunk driving, petty shoplifters, and so-called misdemeanor offenders could be placed in Work and House Arrest or simply cool their heels in the county jail. These options would be available as well for child support and traffic ticket scofflaws.

We have tried everything else -- rehabilitation, in-prison college and training programs -- everything, yet nothing has worked. These new paradigms, especially if publicized, will dramatically reduce recidivism and scare the living bejesus out of potential offenders. Film documentaries of strict regime labor camps would be mandatory viewing at least once a year in every high school in the country. Juvenile boot camps should be the universal norm for juvenile offenders and documentaries detailing life in those facilities would be shown together with films on strict regime labor camps. Strict regime labor camps would probably enjoy wide acceptance among most people today but not among the intellectual and media elite who possess the clout to block it.

Universal DNA Testing

This one should be a no brainer. Mandatory DNA testing of everyone in the United States would go a long way in reducing crime (especially rape) and lessening the chances that innocent people would be convicted of crimes they did not commit. Hundreds of people have been released from wrongful imprisonment when DNA proved their innocence.

All newborns would be tested at birth and every other citizen would be required to submit a DNA sample. It would also be required of foreign nationals with visas authorizing extended stays for work, school, or marriage.

DNA is the best identity tool available today. We would be foolish not to utilize it to its fullest extent and value.

Civil libertarian groups will oppose this on some constitutional ground but if employers can require mandatory drug testing why can't the government snip a strand of hair?

Jury Reform

The present concept of the jury dates back to 13th century English law, which mandated that a "jury of his peers" would try a defendant. This was designed to prevent peasants from being railroaded by the nobility or wealthy landowners. That concept still exists today. Twelve jurors try a person and, in most states, a unanimous verdict is required.

There are two flaws in this process.

Jurors are selected by mailing a summons to registered voters or lists taken from other public records selected at random. It is inconsistent. Some people are called on a regular basis while others never get "drafted." Prospective jurors get out of jury duty through any number of lame excuses. Those who are willing to serve or who cannot come up with an "adequate" excuse are required to report every day or call in for a set period of time. If they don't get selected for a trial they go home and come back or call in the next day -- and the next -- until they are released. This causes minor -- and sometimes major -- disruption in potential jurors' lives both at home and work. If they get selected for a trial of a long duration it causes more disruption in their lives.

Today's legal system is far more complex than that of 13th Century England or even the United States of just a few decades ago. Attorneys on both sides spend time and money cherry picking jurors whom they perceive as favorable to their side. They hire jury selection specialists, which add to the already high cost of the trial. Potential jurors often have to fill out complicated questionnaires about their views on the death penalty and other topics pertaining to that specific trial. Alternates have to be selected as jurors drop out during the course of the trial, which can result in a mistrial. Persuasive arguments and skillful manipulation of evidence by attorneys can easily sway jurors. The O.J. Simpson trial is a textbook case of everything that is wrong with the present jury trial system. The defense did a brilliant job manipulating the jury ("If the glove don't fit, you must acquit.") and playing to the sentiments of a jury that saw in Simpson one of their own. Another example is the exorbitant sums of money awarded in lawsuits such as the woman who was awarded a two million-dollar settlement for spilling a cup of coffee purchased at a fast food restaurant. It was eventually reduced to $480.000.00 -- still too much. But attorneys know how to appeal to the jurors' emotions and sympathies.

My solution is simple: professional jurors. This would still follow the "jury of his peers" concept as these jurors would be citizen volunteers. Upon volunteering and, after being screened and selected, they would undergo a training course covering such topics as how to discern evidence and acquiring some knowledge and familiarity with basic legal principles and terminology. Being a juror would not be a job or a career but a volunteer position for which they would be paid a reasonable stipend and per diem including meals and lodging if necessary. They would be guaranteed by law administrative leave from their jobs without penalty but this is something that would probably attract a lot of retired people. Government employees would be likely candidates since government agencies would be more likely to be willing to give the jurors the time needed.

Instead of twelve jurors, this paradigm calls for five. They would still have to reach a unanimous verdict. In trials with a racial component, the jury would need to be racially balanced. At least two jurors would be of the defendant's gender, racial, or ethnic background.

This plan would eliminate the inconvenience and expense of sending out summons to prospective jurors and dealing with their excuses. Since all jurors would be pre-screened as a requirement for selection as a volunteer juror, they could be selected at random by the Court thus eliminating "cherry picking" (except, perhaps, in cases involving juror opposition to the death penalty). Trials would be of shorter duration since lawyers would not sense much value in theatrics, showmanship, and melodramatic arguments with a trained professional jury. There would be less chance of jurors dropping out or being replaced in the middle of the trial. It could provide de facto tort reform as trained professionals would be less apt to award outlandish litigation settlements. It would provide for fairer verdicts in an era of increasing legal complexity.

It is time to try something new in jury formation.

Restructuring the Military

Our present military system is a throwback not only to World War II but to the 19th Century Indian wars as well. The system of forts -- the word itself conjures up images of old John Wayne movies -- dates back to an army fighting warring Indian tribes and offering a safe haven for settlers and travelers making their way across the country. Today they are political footballs and pork barrels designed to boost the economy of congressional districts and get senators and representatives re-elected. Why does San Antonio, TX need three Air Force Bases (Lackland, Brooks, and Randolph) an Army post -- Fort Sam Houston -- and two military hospitals -- Wilford Hall (Air Force) and Brooke Army Medical Center. Washington State has a naval homeport in Everett, a naval submarine base at Bangor, and the Puget Sound Naval Shipyard in Bremerton, virtually next door to Bangor. Fifty miles north of Everett is Whidbey Island Naval Air Station. Forty miles from Bremerton, outside Tacoma, we have McChord AFB and Fort Lewis (currently known as Joint Base Lewis-McChord).

The majority of uniformed military personnel do not perform combat duties; instead, they are personnel, and administrative staff, mechanics, truck drivers and a host of other pencil pushing and wrench bending jobs that could and should be performed by civilians. Civilians should perform all support functions that do not involve the use of a weapon.

The Marine Corps is obsolete. They were originally intended to take and hold beaches; instead, they have evolved into an ersatz army.

We no longer need large standing armies. The focus is now on special operations and counter-insurgency. We have the technology to destroy large troop concentrations from miles away or miles above. What we need on the ground is an army of 50,000 men. I say *men* because most women do not have the physical strength and capability to meet the training requirements this elite force would have to pass -- a combination of the Navy Seals, the Army Delta Force and the French Foreign Legion. All soldiers would be airborne qualified, undersea qualified, and trained to fight in all types of climate and terrain. They would be familiar with all basic weaponry and some would specialize in higher tech weapons such as missile defense technology. They would be totally self-sufficient in combat with no support or rear guard troops except for medics. These troops would be used primarily for overseas military operations and only fight on U.S. soil in the event of an invasion of the North American Continent.

15

We cannot be isolationist. What happens anywhere on the globe affects us here in the United States. Consider the consequences to the world -- and to the United States -- if Iran is allowed to develop nuclear weapons or if Saddam Hussein had conquered all of the Persian Gulf oil states in 1990 thereby taking over three-fifths of the world's oil supply. It would have resulted in a worldwide 1930s style Depression. Only United States leadership prevented this from happening.

The New Paradigm Army would consist of five divisions. These divisions would be divided up among the different combat specialties as determined by the Department of Defense. This force would be based in a thinly populated region – possibly Montana or somewhere in the desert southwest or Texas. This installation would include an Air Wing so troops could be deployed to any destination on earth within 72 hours -- or less.

There would have to be incentives to attract and retain qualified personnel. These incentives should be enough to keep a soldier for a full 20 - 30 year career. To ensure a qualified force, each applicant would be rigorously tested and screened physically, psychologically and mentally. Successful applicants would be given a $25,000.00 tax-free enlistment bonus payable upon successful completion of Basic and and advanced training for a five-year enlistment. Subsequent re-enlistment bonuses would be $35000.00 tax-free. Retirement would include a $75,000.00 tax-free "golden handshake" followed by a lifetime pension. **(Author's Note: These amounts could vary depending upon economic conditions.)** Monthly pay for all grades would be at a professional level; all New Paradigm Army pay and retirement would be tax-free. Retirees and dependents would have full medical insurance coverage at no cost to them. A certain percentage of non-citizens would be allowed to enlist and would be eligible to receive United States citizenship upon the successful completion of their first enlistment.

We need a college educated officer corps in today's high tech and ever changing world. The New Paradigm Army would have a four-year Academy but there would be no more ROTC. ROTC stands for Reserve Officers Training Corps. It was designed to create Reserve officers and, while many ROTC graduates did earn regular commissions, it would not be a suitable conduit for the kind of Army envisioned in this paradigm. ROTC has become obsolete. In the Army, non-Academy college graduate future officers would enter the service by attending enlisted basic training and serve at least two years as an enlisted soldier.   All combat training would be completed while in enlisted status.   Afterwards, they would enter Officer Training

School for a six-month course. Successful completion would earn the candidate a commission as a second lieutenant. Washouts would return to the enlisted ranks without prejudice to complete the remainder of their enlistment and be eligible for re-enlistment under the usual conditions of honorable service.

The concept is to create a thoroughly professional career Army. The public, knowing that these men were well-paid professionals, would be less inclined to wring its hands in a "bring the boys home, cut and run" frenzy when things get tough. But along with this New Paradigm Army would be a new paradigm strategy of "in-and-out" operations; no prolonged stays and no more "nation building." The longer we stay the more mired down we get. That is currently (as of this writing) the case in Afghanistan. It was the case in Iraq and in Vietnam before that. We never seem to accomplish our objectives with long stays since objectives seem to change and become blurred over time. The paradigm calls for a clearly defined objective followed by quick and precise execution and speedy departure.

This paradigm would take several years to phase in. During this phase in period we would have to make temporary concessions to areas such as officer training.

The Air Force would focus on air combat operations -- both conventional flying and drones -- air transport, and missile operations. The administrative and maintenance components would be handled by civilians. All uniformed Air Force personnel would be officers with college degrees. They would be trained in a program similar to the old Aviation Cadet program beginning with Officer Training School and then pilot training. Missile launch officers would attend a separate training after graduation from Officer Training School and commissioning. Terms of service and compensation would be the same as the New Paradigm Army.

Like the Marine Corps, the Navy, with the exception of the submarine service, has become obsolete. Any function battleships and destroyers perform can be done from the air. Cruise missiles can be launched just as effectively from aircraft as ships. Submarines can fire missiles and blockade harbors. Under this paradigm it would be necessary to expand our submarine service. Non-nuclear weapons could be deployed using an ever-advancing drone technology. The days of the armada vs armada battles (e.g., Midway in World War II) are gone. Civilians can handle seaborne transport functions. The argument against using civilians to transport troops and materials into war zones is trumped by the fact that civilian shipping is always going into war zones. A contract Merchant Marine is the solution to the transportation issue.

A separate submarine service would be part of the Army and Air Force with the same terms of service and compensation. It would have both officers and enlisted personnel and a service academy. Non-academy officers would serve at least two years as enlisted personnel and then attend a six month officer training   program. A commission would require a college degree. This super-service (Army, Submarine Service and Air Force) would be under one central command. This concept will meet with a lot of resistance since tradition is so embedded in our military. But in today's world we need a rapid professional response with no inter-service rivalry, bickering, or politics. This force would be heavily standardized.

Our primary waterborne force would be an expanded Coast Guard since we need capability to intervene in our territorial waters to interdict illegal maritime traffic and contraband. "Territorial Waters" should extend to 200 miles in the Atlantic and Pacific Oceans. Territorial limits in the Caribbean would have to be negotiated with the other sovereign nations in the region. We would have to negotiate with Canada regarding territorial waters between Alaska and Washington State.

We would no longer have military bases overseas. This is another Cold War holdover. It costs too much money and is part of the reason why Europe has become pacifist. Why emphasize national defense when Uncle Sam is always there to bail them out as we did in two world wars and throughout the Cold War. It's time to end that dependency. All U.S. military would be based in the United States. To make this happen we need to develop rapid deployment and rapid response. There is no reason why we cannot develop ultra-long-range high-speed aircraft capable of circumnavigating the earth at two to three thousand mph without refueling. The Japanese and Italians were developing long-range engine technology during World War II. This would eliminate the need for overseas bases and aircraft carriers. We could base *temporarily* overseas if necessary.

This paradigm would meet with considerable opposition since it defies conventional wisdom and traditions dating back to the foundation of the United States. But this is the 21st Century and large standing armies of citizen soldiers are obsolete in an era of high tech wars that requires a quick, professional response before international incidents escalate out of control into a nuclear and global confrontation. This highly skilled state-of-the-art techno-military 50,000 man force augmented by its air and submarine branches, could handle the few nations that have large standing armies (China, Russia and North Korea). Bodies don't win wars; skill and technology do.

We need to rid ourselves of World War II style strategies. The military is as stuck in this rut as the WWI generals were in charging enemy positions with large numbers of troops. That methodology was fine when the main weapon was the single shot musket but machine guns, tanks, and artillery rendered that strategy obsolete. The World War II strategy served us well up until Vietnam but became obsolete with the advent of advanced air operations and missile technology. If the terrorists re-build their camps in Afghanistan after we leave, it will be fairly simple and cost effective to take them out with missiles that could be launched from the United States. Prolonged "search and destroy" ground operations are costly in lives and money. Take care of the problem with precision air strikes and let the locals clean up the mess on their dime.

Homeland Defense

We would use the National Guard for homeland defense but its role needs to be expanded into the following arenas:

- **Provide security for airports and seaports.**
- **Patrol the borders.**
- **Quell civil disturbances (riots)**
- **Provide rapid response disaster relief (hurricanes, earthquakes, floods etc.)**

The National Guard would be called the State Militia, a title more in keeping with its role as envisioned by the Founding Fathers. It would remain under state authority but since it would be dealing with border, airport, and seaport security it would receive some federal funding in payment for assisting the Federal Government in performing Federal functions. Individual State militias could not be utilized outside the geographic borders of their states unless the North American continent was under foreign invasion or to augment another State Militia in an emergency. In the case of foreign invasion they would serve under the direct command of the New Paradigm Army. States could have the power to draft their citizens into the State Militia. A citizen could only be drafted into the militia of his/her state of official residence. Draftees would serve two years of active duty followed by two years active reserve duty and two years inactive reserve duty. Enlistees would serve three years of active duty followed by three years inactive reserve duty. **(Author's Note: The New Paradigm Army would have no Reserve component.)** All Reserve duty would be preceded by an active duty tour. Twenty to thirty year careers would be available in the Militia.

College graduates could earn a commission after serving at least one year active enlisted duty. They would then attend a three-month Officer Training School followed by a four year service obligation.

This paradigm would do away with the Air National Guard since it was not part of the original State Militia concept. Since the State Militia would be operating within the confines of their state the need for air transport would be minimal and, when needed, could be chartered. The State Militia would have a helicopter and small aircraft component but larger airlift requirements would be handled by charter.

A New Concept of Public Education

Nearly everyone agrees that public education in the United States is in trouble. There is a lack of discipline and respect for teachers. We have some of the lowest standardized test scores in Math and Science in the industrialized world. We have to import doctors, nurses, scientists, and technicians. One factor that I see on a regular basis is the unbelievable ignorance of recent history among the Millennial generation. Jay Leno on *The Tonight Show*, had a feature in which he asks college students questions such as what countries did we fight in World War II or who is the current vice-president? Most of them are clueless. *The O'Reilly Factor* has a similar feature and you can find more on You Tube.

Math and Science are worse.

There have been a lot of studies and theorizing about why American public education is in such a mess. The best known of these is *A Nation at Risk* published in 1983. It has not gone out of date. On the contrary, it has "updated" itself.

In this paradigm we will look at a part of the problem that has been largely overlooked: **that the current paradigm of American education is out-of-date**. American public education is operating on a 19th century concept of the "whole-person, well-rounded" student. It was probably based on the idea of the "Renaissance Man." And, at that time, it was workable. Until the World War I era, most high school students were highly intelligent and capable of mastering a variety of subjects and academic disciplines. Secondary education and beyond was a luxury. Today a high school diploma is no longer a luxury, it is a necessity. Today the system no longer serves Renaissance men -- and women; instead, it caters to a large and intellectually diverse student population with a wide variety of interests and abilities. The current educational system does not recognize these differences. The result is that many intelligent students are bored, drop out, or never achieve their full academic potential. A lot of student failure is blamed on non-academic issues such as the breakdown of the family and drugs. These are part of the overall problem but a curriculum that could grab and hold a student's interest could be their salvation from these outside negative influences.

Thomas Armstrong developed a concept which appears in *Multiple Intelligences In The Classroom* which was published in 1994. Armstrong identified eight different types of intelligences, six of which could form the basis for a solid academic curriculum. Following is his analysis of these six intelligences:

Linguistic Intelligence

Students with this type of intelligence enjoy writing and reading. They enjoy good conversation and have excellent recall of names, dates and places. They are good spellers and have a solid command of their native language. Communication skills, written and verbal, predominate.

Subjects of interest: English, foreign languages, History, Creative Writing, Sociology, Anthropology, Current Events, Religion, Philosophy.

Logical-Mathematical Intelligence

These students excel at mathematics and enjoy math and computer games. They are good at "figuring things out." People in this category have well-developed analytical skills and know how to ask the right questions. They like chess, checkers, and other games of strategy. They function well in the abstract and are able to understand cause and effect relationships.

Subjects of interest: Mathematics, Physics, Chemistry, Engineering, Architecture, Computer Science, Technology, Statistics, Logic, Law, Philosophy, Accounting, Economics. Medicine and Psychology.

Naturalistic Intelligence

Enjoy being in the outdoors. Have a knowledge and interest in plants, animals, and insects and can identify them. These people enjoy gardening and yard work, fishing, hunting, and camping.

Subjects of interest: Biology, Zoology, Animal Husbandry, Agriculture, Landscaping, and Forestry.

Musical Intelligence

These students have a natural inclination toward music. They can play one or more instruments, have an ear for tone, rhythm, and beat. They enjoy singing to themselves, listening to music, and composing their own music and lyrics. They can identify singers and are usually walking encyclopedias of musical history and trivia. They like to dance since it requires a sense of rhythm and beat.

Subjects of interest: Music (including instrument playing) and Dance

Spatial Intelligence

These People can visualize.. They have a propensity towards art because of their natural sense of proportion and dimension. They are good at putting together puzzles. They enjoy movies and photography since these are visual communications. They can manipulate three-dimensional figures in their minds. Design of any kind is their specialty.

Subjects of interest: similar to those in the Logical-Mathematical category to which we could add Photography, motion pictures, and Geography (specializing in map-making and latitudinal and longitudinal studies).

Bodily-Kinesthetic Intelligence

These students are interested in sports, physical activities, and are good with their hands. They are mechanically inclined and good at fixing and repairing things. Other skills include theater and dancing.

Subjects of interest: Physical Education, Vehicle Repair, Woodshop and Building classes, Drama, and Dancing.

All schools need to teach grammar, mathematics (up to pre-Algebra), History, Geography, Writing and Communications Skills. These classes would be taught in grades 1 - 8 and be reinforced through continuing education throughout high school. But does every student need to know Algebra, Geometry, and Calculus? Does every student need to be well versed in the great western writers? Does everyone need to know a foreign language? Does everyone need to be able to write a term paper on the finer points of the New Deal? Do all students have to memorize the Valence chart? Of course not. Force feeding these subjects to students who have little or no interest or aptitude for them cause boredom, dissatisfaction and, in too many cases, dropping out.

Teach a basic curriculum, as outlined in the last paragraph, through grades one to eight and then assess students to see what their interests, aptitudes, and abilities really are. Based on the results set up a high school curriculum based on whichever intelligence matches their skills.

We need to return to the old Grade school (grades 1 through 8) and high school (grades 9-12). Get rid of junior highs, middle schools, primary schools, intermediate schools, and any other such combinations. These are more political than educational since they keep more teachers and administrators employed. There should be two missions: Grade school teaching a solid grounding in the basics and high school focusing on the natural aptitudes and abilities of the individual student.

The Public Education system needs to encourage, promote, and provide incentives and standards to students to major in the sciences and foreign languages; not only Spanish and French but Arabic, Farsi (Persian) Russian, Chinese, and Korean -- even Urdu, Tajiki and Uzbeki. One of the reasons why the Russians were successful during the Cold War era was their emphasis on language. Every officer in the Russian military can read, write, and speak fluent English. The ambassador and consular level officers at every Russian embassy and consulate around the world are fluent in the language of the host country. We need the same skills. Every American military officer should be able to read, speak, and write at least one of the following languages: Arabic, Russian, Korean, Chinese, and Farsi. In today's complex world we need specialists -- not "Renaissance men and women."

Life skills need to be embedded into the curriculum -- stress management, anger management, financial management, time management, career planning, parenting skills -- the skills needed to function successfully in today's world.

Now what about the Millennials that don't know the name of the vice-president? These are issues more of *cultural literacy* than pure history. William Bennett wrote a book called *Cultural Literacy* which outlined what every culturally literate American should know. The schools need to teach this beginning with First Grade all the way through Grade 12. Cultural Literacy needs to have its own class hour built into the curriculum every day. Students do not need to know the details of every battle in World War II but they need to know which countries were involved, the years it spanned, the key figures, and the causes and effects of the war that we are still feeling down to the present day.

Education is a necessity for economic survival in today's world. People without high school level education will seldom rise above minimum wage jobs. The time is coming when no employer will hire anyone without a high school diploma or GED. But for education to be successful we have to teach to the student's natural aptitudes and skills. Trying to cram Algebra down a historian's throat or vice versa is often a formula for failure.

There are a number of excellent interest and aptitude tests e.g., *The World of Work Inventory* (WOWI) which can guide students toward intelligent career planning. Most of us can learn how to do most jobs. We succeed or fail in jobs or careers based upon the compatibility between our personalities and our work.

Lastly, school attendance needs to be mandatory until graduation or age 19 (not 18), whichever comes first. Some students drop out because the schools they attend are out of control. Discipline has to be restored in schools. Chronically disruptive students or those who pose a threat to others should be put in Boot Camp alternative day schools where they would be taught in a boot camp environment. These schools would be separated by gender. Students who don't cooperate in Boot Camp school will be in violation of civil (and perhaps criminal) statutes and could be sentenced to Boot Camp Reformatory (See "All Time is Hard Time") possibly until age 21. We really need to get serious about education in this country.

Another reason why students fail in school is the lack of motivation. They can fail even in subjects that could interest them if the teacher cannot motivate. The movie *Stand and Deliver* told the story of Jaime Escalante, a teacher in a barrio school in Los Angeles during the 1970s. His students were Hispanics who had been written off as too dumb to learn and were simply being "warehoused." Escalante took them up to Calculus. They took the Advanced Placement (AP) test and most scored 4s or 5s, five being the highest possible score. Educational Testing Service, the company that creates the AP tests suspected cheating and retested them under strict controls. All passed with the same or better score. No student scored below 3 on either test. Jaime Escalante was an excellent teacher and even better motivator.

High Tech Voting

Over the past couple of presidential elections we have heard much about election fraud -- felons voting, dead people voting, hanging chads, dimpled chads, voting machines dating back to the Grover Cleveland presidency, minorities being denied access to polls etc. etc. etc. ad nauseam.   Here in Washington State in the 2004 gubernatorial election the Republican candidate initially won by 42 (forty-two) votes statewide. After two recounts with obvious political shenanigans (one precinct in Seattle tuned in more votes than there were registered voters), the Democratic candidate won. In the 2000 presidential election the Democrats were unwilling to concede the election to George Bush based on a razor thin margin in a few counties in Florida. Voting methods vary from state to state. Some states use punch cards, others use voting booths and an increasing number send out absentee ballots, which are highly vulnerable to fraud. Absentee ballots are too often cast by deceased voters and not from Heaven either. Families do not report deaths to the local election authorities so it is possible for one person to send in two (sometimes more) votes.

There has to be a better way. And there is. Voters would cast their votes using their telephone keypads. They would punch in their Social Security number and a five-to-eight digit pin number using a touch-tone phone. Voters would need to register their Social Security number and establish a pin number. This information would be encrypted on a secure computer under the supervision of the county election authority with simple prompts instructing each voter exactly how to register. Illiterate voters and those with disabilities that might pose a barrier to this system could have a designated "Representative voter" on file with the local election authority with notarized permission to cast their ballots for them. The "Representative Voter" could register for them. The voter and the representative would both have to register in person.

The pin number could not be their birth day or address. It could not contain consecutive numbers but it could include the pound sign (#) and the star key (*).   On Election Day, the voter would access a toll free number.   Each state and the District of Columbia would have its own phone number. Overseas voters would have an international toll free number. Voting hours would be 5 A.M. – 8 P.M. local. Overseas voters would have to call during the hours their home states were open for voting.

Here is how the process would work: Each voter would enter their Social Security Number and pin plus 5 digit Zip Code. The Zip Code would activate the proper ballot. Each candidate on the slate would be assigned a number. For example: to vote for John Smith, press 1; to vote for Jane Doe, press 2. If the number of candidates exceeded 9, the voter would push two digits and the pound sign (10#). On initiatives and referendums the voter would press 1 for yes and 2 for no. The system would verify each Social Security number and pin number once per election cycle to ensure the voter was still alive, had not moved, was not in jail etc.

This system would eliminate virtually all of the problems listed above including people voting using the names of deceased relatives. Next of kin would be required by law to notify the local election authority when a relative passes away. They already have to notify the Social Security Administration and other retirement and pension programs. There could be a cross referencing system to facilitate this.

Billions of dollars would have to be invested in this system and, with sufficient safeguards and back-up safeguards, the hacking risk would be minimized. There would be no website and no information available on any Internet search engine.

No system is perfect and this one is no exception but it is in keeping with state-of-the-art technology, something the current archaic and inconsistent voting methods are not. The key word is *standardization*. This new paradigm would eliminate fiascoes like the 2000 presidential election and the 2004 Washington State gubernatorial election.

The Making of the President

I borrowed the title of this paradigm from the series of books by Theodore White detailing the presidential campaigns of the 1960s and early 1970s. A more appropriate title for recent campaigns might *be The Breaking of the President*. Modern presidential campaigns are too long and this reduces them to sideshows and the candidates to pathetic laughingstocks: Michael Dukakis on the tank trying to look like George Patton; Gary Bauer flipping that pancake into nowhere. (I don't think it was ever found); John Kerry in that ridiculous goose hunting expedition that symbolized his bid for the presidency -- a wild goose chase; the Dean Scream; and, taking it back to 1972, the Muskie cry. All of the candidates try to cultivate a "guy-next-door" image. Dukakis wanted everyone to know that he drove a Plymouth Reliant. Well, you don't get much more guy-next-door than that. Presidential candidates should have learned from Adlai Stevenson's ridiculous attempt back in 1956 to be "just plain folks." There was a television commercial showing him carrying a bag of groceries into the house and "inviting us in." Adlai Stevenson, and all of the other candidates since, would be as lost in a supermarket as a caveman in a computer store. George H.W. Bush proved that when he tried to be "just plain folks" doing some family grocery shopping and was totally blown away by the barcode scanner that had replaced the traditional cash register. Presidential campaigns have become national -- and now with cable and satellite TV -- international jokes. Who can take these people seriously after all the humiliating fraternity boy style hazing of the primaries?

Drop the primaries.

They consume too much time and money putting the candidates heavily in debt to the special interests that pay for all this nonsense. The primary debates often descend into verbal food fights loaded with personal attacks between the candidates and "gotcha" questions from the moderators. Let the convention go back to its original purpose and decide the nominee. The convention has become an expensive rubber stamp for the candidate that survives (and I do mean *survives*) the primaries.

Candidates will announce their candidacy no earlier than six months before the convention. During this time the candidates can do everything they need to get their messages out. The parties can pay polling companies to track the candidates. Every candidate will be given one hour to outline their campaign platform at the convention and then let the delegates decide. This may not seem democratic but we are a Republic which means we have *representative* government and the delegates *represent* their party's constituents. After the convention, the winning candidates will have two months to campaign. After the convention, each candidate will receive three hours of government funded air time and three televised debates. In addition, each candidate will receive an equal amount of federal funding to carry their campaigns to Election Day. After the convention candidates will not receive any outside funding. They will have to make do with their federal campaign allowances. This would cut down on travel but with television, the internet and social media, big rallies have become redundant. In a nation of well over 300 million people, how many people can a candidate really touch in personal appearances?

Third-party candidates would campaign with the party that most closely matches their own political philosophy. All political positions are covered within the framework of the two main parties and there is no need for a third party. History has proven third parties to be futile. If a candidate refuses to affiliate with one of the two parties, they will pay for their campaign out of their own pocket; but if they have any sense of history, they will realize the futility in that.

This is not a perfect solution by any means and, in all honesty, it is the weakest paradigm in the book but it would cut down on the election cycle (which seems to begin right after Inauguration day), the exorbitant amounts of money being spent, and it would force the candidates to focus on issues especially after the conventions when there would not be enough money to waste on personal attacks, an all too common feature of today's presidential elections. It would go a long way in alleviating "Election Fatigue" which I feel generates voter burnout. The electorate starts "tuning out" and this can result in a poor choice on Election Day.

Streamlining State and Local Governments

There are three state and local (county and municipal) functions that overlap. They could be combined under one umbrella to maximize efficiency and minimize redundancy. They are: the Police, the Courts, and revenue collection.

The Police

All states have at least three levels of police: State (sometimes called the Highway Patrol), county, and city. City police lack jurisdiction outside the city limits. The County Sheriff's Department has no jurisdiction inside the incorporated towns and cities within the county that have their own local police forces. The State Patrol is limited to the state highways and the interstate system within the state.

Put them all under the State so any police officer would have jurisdiction anywhere in the State. Abolish the Highway (or State) Patrol) and incorporate it into what would be called , for example, the Washington State Police Department presided over by a commissioner appointed by the governor. The only area where the State Police Department would not have jurisdiction would be tribal Reservations. Joint agreements could be developed with tribal police to deal with inter-jurisdictional issues.

The old paradigm made sense when local communities were more isolated. Today, with metropolitan regions running into each other connected by super highways and computer technology, it makes sense to put the police under one central authority.

The Courts

Courts face the same jurisdictional limitations as the Police. Municipal Courts, District Courts, and Superior Courts would be replaced by State Courts presided over by judges who would hold statewide jurisdiction. Today, if you live in Tacoma and have a court issue, even a traffic ticket, in Spokane, you have to travel across the state to deal with it. Under this New Paradigm, a judge in Tacoma could adjudicate a Spokane traffic ticket. Judges would be appointed by the governor and approved by the Legislature. Why should some judges be appointed and others elected? Electing judges makes no real sense since most people don't know anything about judicial candidates and just pick one at random. I never vote for a judicial candidate unless I know something about them, which is rare.

State Revenues

Under the current system we have city, county, and state taxes. Take the cities and counties out of the tax collecting business and let the State run it. This paradigm would provide for a uniform rate of taxation statewide. The one- percent Property taxes collected would be allocated to the counties in which they were collected. Sales taxes would be standardized throughout the state and returned to the counties in which they were collected.

Some functions should remain under local control i.e., Public Utilities and School Districts. Utility resources should have utilization priority in those regions of the state where they are produced and not siphoned off by state bureaucrats to other regions for political purposes. Local Public Utilities would be free to make their own decisions whether or not to sell water and electricity to other areas inside or outside the state.

Public schools are set up to meet local needs. Different parts of the state have different population groups with different and diverse needs. All school districts in the state are under the aegis of the State School Superintendent while retaining the autonomy to make decisions to meet local needs.

The main objection to his paradigm is that things are best handled at the local level -- a form of the Principle of Subsidiarity which says that all functions should be handled at the lowest administrative level possible. Yes, but not if it involves incredible amounts of duplication and redundancy.

A New Economic Paradigm

The American economy is in trouble. We have no real industrial base in this country anymore. The steel industry is a shadow of its former self. The American automobile industry has trouble competing with Japanese and European car makers. Most of our electronic merchandise comes from Asia.. We do build computers and airplanes but an increasing amount of the parts and labor are outsourced to India, China, Latin America, and Southeast Asia. Our educational system is not producing enough engineers, scientists, technicians, and doctors so we have to import them from overseas. When the Republicans bragged about the low unemployment rate in the early 2000s, the Democrats counter by describing most of these jobs as "hamburger flipping jobs". They're right but the same can be said of the "booming economy" during the Democratic Clinton Administration. We have been stuck in a "Service Economy" model for decades. The cost of gasoline is unstable. Housing costs are out of reach of many people even after the 2008 meltdown. Personal debt is out of control.

So how do we fix this mess?

Implement a Policy of National self-sufficiency.

(Author's Note: None of what follows implies support for Isolationism. We are part of a global economy but we cannot DEPEND on any foreign source for vital resources, technology, expertise, or even luxury items. Most importantly, we cannot continue to depend on foreign loans to keep our government functioning. The following 11 point plan would end this dependency while making us more self-sufficient both as a nation and as individuals.)

1. *Energy Self-Sufficiency*

We have made enormous progress in this area in recent years largely thanks to "fracking." But we need to do more. We must exploit ALL of our oil, coal (which can be turned into petroleum) and natural gas resources and form a North American cartel to replace OPEC as the world's primary supplier of oil and natural gas. This would give us tremendous economic and political leverage. It would put us in a position to exercise control over hostile nations like Russia and Iran whose economies depend in large part on oil exports. This would also release Western Europe from reliance and dependence on regimes that could try to control them though the "oil weapon" and oil is a weapon as we found out during the Energy

Crisis in the early 1970s. Energy self-sufficiency would give us international political and economic clout and we could use oil as a way of reducing our national debt as we will discuss later.

We need to update our power grid to protect it both from solar flares and electromagnetic pulse attacks from hostile powers. We must develop solar power as our primary generator of electricity and phase in other alternative forms of energy. This will take time to accomplish if we are to do it sensibly and efficiently. We could neutralize oil company opposition by letting them develop it since they have the money and resources to do it.

Energy self-sufficiency (including effective alternative energy models) is now in reach. For those who say we cannot possibly accomplish this, let me point out some historical projects that they said couldn't be done either.

- Building a Navy that would hand the Japanese a crushing defeat (Midway) within six months of Pearl Harbor.
- The Manhattan Project to build the atomic bomb.
- Carrying out President Kennedy's mandate of putting astronauts on the moon by the end of the 1960s.
- South Africa was able to attain self-sufficiency during Apartheid with far less resources than the United States.

We had to build the technology for the Manhattan Project and interplanetary space travel from scratch. For energy self-sufficiency we already have the technology so let's develop it and put it to work.

2. *Re-industrialization*

One of the effects of globalization has been the loss of our industrial base. Following World War II until the 1960s we were the ONLY fully operational industrial economy in the world. The primary causes of American industrial decline are the high cost of American labor coupled with a hostile taxation system and the adversarial relationship between business and government. This has led to business stifling over-regulation. Historically, the Republicans were perceived as letting business get away with anything while the Democrats over tax and over regulate. While these perceptions were not altogether true, neither were they altogether false. And there is the issue of quality. Foreign products, especially automobiles, are simply better than their American counterparts. They say that patriotism is the last refuge of the scoundrel; it is also the last refuge of the substandard manufacturer. I like to think that I would die for my country but there is no way I'd buy an American car. What is left of American industry does everything on the cheap. In fairness, there is some progress toward improvement but Japanese and German cars are still better as sales indicate.

There must be an active partnership between government and business. Re-industrialization is necessarily a part of national self-sufficiency -- and national security. We need to re-build the steel industry, the electronics industry, the shipbuilding industry, the manufacturing industry (we don't even make toys here anymore), the garment industry, and improve the automobile industry. The Government should make interest free loans available and grant a three year tax holiday to these new businesses. Discourage outsourcing through a combination of tax incentives and fines. 15 percent would be the ordinary corporate tax.

(Author's Note: Government loans for re-industrialization would have to be approved by Congress in public hearings and the loan applicants would have to present a comprehensive and detailed business plan that would be public information. In other words -- no White House loans to big campaign donors.)

The biggest obstacle to a realistic re-industrialization program would be the Labor Unions since we cannot implement re-industrialization if we have to pay excessive wages and benefits. This is going to involve sacrifice and, as of this writing, it appears that the public has no stomach for sacrifice.

3. *Re-building the Small Business Base*

I'm old enough to remember the corner grocery store, the "five-and-dime", the family farm, little hole-in-the-wall restaurants and cafes (my mother owned one of these), and a host of the other "mom and pop" business that have all but disappeared from the American landscape. They've been replaced by chains, conglomerates, and franchises most of which are housed in sterile shopping malls. While these mega-stores are not legally constituted as monopolies, they are de facto monopolies as they stifle small business competition. The mom and pops cannot compete. And there is more to it than merely an economic effect. These little businesses defined the American neighborhood. When we lost them we lost part of the essence of the American neighborhood.

National self-sufficiency requires the restoration of that small neighborhood business base. State and Federal governments would provide seed money in the form of interest free loans together with a three year Federal Tax holiday -- exactly the same package new corporations would get under Re-industrialization. States with small populations could offer financing to start small businesses to entrepreneurs from outside the local area if they would move there and set up shop.

Like Re-industrialization, this would take some setting up but it would stimulate the competition needed to bring prices down. These big conglomerates are de facto monopolies and this is equally the case in agribusiness. Conglomerates like Arthur Daniels and Conagra control much of it. Smaller family farms would also help reduce the dependence on illegal aliens since the family would do much of the work that is presently outsourced to illegals.

These loans would have to be re-paid under the Law. They are not subsidies. Businesses that default on their Federal or state loans would be subject to re-possession and foreclosure and the government would sell these businesses on the free market.

People do not value something-for-nothing grants and subsidies. It makes them feel "entitled" thereby destroying the work ethic that is a crucial part of National Re-industrialization.

4. *Re-evaluate the Minimum Wage*

The Minimum Wage will always be a poverty level wage whether it is $1.00 per hour or $100.00 per hour. It is meant for the least skilled workers and will keep prices of goods and services artificially high. When the Minimum Wage is increased everything goes up in price. Skilled workers demand more and to pay labor costs, businesses have to raise prices. This inflates the currency and causes layoffs, downsizing, and outsourcing. It is a vicious economic circle. Reduce the minimum wage as far down as the market will bear. A Free Market Economy always finds the median point.

The immediate result would be the elimination of the need to outsource. Prices would readjust to meet wage scales.

On the other end of the wage spectrum we need to eliminate the so-called "Prevailing Wage." Repeal the Davis-Bacon Act that created it. The Prevailing Wage often prices American labor out of the market and greatly (and artificially) increases the costs of building and construction which is passed on to the buyer, the consumer, and the taxpayer. Government contracts are required by law to pay Prevailing Wage (The Davis-Bacon Act). This has an especially adverse effect on economically depressed areas.

The effects of these wages (Minimum and Prevailing) reverberate throughout the entire economy raising the cost of everything from a pack of chewing gum to the construction of a new shopping mall and everything in between.

High minimum wages are inflationary and this is no more evident than in the restaurant industry. Prices and layoffs increase as soon as the Minimum Wage goes up. There would be painful adjustments at first but *the Free Market always* **finds the median** and that is the central theme of these new economic paradigms. Yes, they are painful at first but cures very often are painful.

None of this will happen in the current political climate dominated as it is by Organized Labor and vote hungry politicians.

(AUTHOR'S NOTE: Since I first wrote this, Seattle, Washington has raised its minimum wage to $15.00 an hour. Employees began requesting less hours since the increase was causing reductions in their government benefits (Food Stamps, subsidized housing and child care); yet another unintended consequence.)

5. *Rapid Transit*

This is simpler than it looks. We need to abandon our focus on new light rail construction because it is not cost effective. The cost and disruption involved in digging tunnels and tearing up heavily populated areas cannot be justified. Neither is the amount of time it takes. The answer is buses -- lots and lots of them. They could be purchased and on the road within days. Unlike rail that has to go where the tracks are, buses could be re-routed as needed to meet demand. Most of the newer buses run on natural gas so pollution is not an issue. This would take minimal (comparatively speaking) planning and implementation.

For intra and interstate transportation we should copy Europe's and Japan's rail systems and introduce bullet trains. As of this writing we have zero bullet trains in the United States; yet 200 – 300 mph trains are feasible.   The only obstacle would be crossings in towns and cities. In Europe they use overpasses to get around this problem. Still, there are large parts of the nation where this is not a problem and for those few and far between population centers, the trains could slow down.   A transcontinental 300-mph bullet train could travel from coast to coast, stops included, in 12 hours or less.

Rebuild the traditional railroad system to facilitate the shipment of goods. It would be cheaper, save energy, and get a lot of trucks off the highways. We already have the infrastructure in place to do that. But it needs upgrading and repair.

6. *Getting Medical Costs Under Control*

United States citizens pay more for medical care than any other country in the world and they are increasing by 15 percent every year. . If you ever ask a hospital to send you an itemized statement, which they must provide upon request, you will find aspirin and Tylenol capsules cost up to $2.00 each. That, of course, is only the beginning. My mother's last week in the hospital came to more than $18,000.00. That was for just lying in bed and getting a few pills and IVs. Doctors, hospitals, and nursing homes charge these exorbitant prices because Medicare, Medicaid, and wealthy insurance companies with deep pockets cover the majority of the population in one way or another. It has become a vicious circle as private insurance companies then raise their rates as Medicare and Medicaid cut back. Health insurance is a big part of company paid employee benefits. There is no end in sight to cost increases. We regularly read about Medicare and Medicaid fraud, which only serves to increase costs. For instance, when my aunt went into the hospital on a Sunday, she was diagnosed and admitted with bronchitis. The next day, Monday, her primary care physician re-diagnosed her with pneumonia since physicians can bill Medicare at a higher rate for pneumonia than bronchitis. At the time, she was in an advanced stage of chronic congestive heart failure and pneumonia would have killed her. Another favorite practice is to keep the patient in the hospital for a few days and then ship them off to a nursing home. How necessary is this?

So how do we deal with this national fiasco? In 1994, Hillary Clinton set about to reform medical insurance. That failed because the essence of her plan was to shift costs around. It was a combination of a shell game and a Ponzi scheme. It failed to investigate WHY medical costs are so high. This was a major failing of Obamacare in 2010 which, unlike Hillarycare, was shoved down the national throat by Presidential and Congressional fiat. Medical facilities come up with all kinds of excuses such as the need to make up the cost of treatment for those who cannot pay.

Here is the solution:

The President should appoint a commission to investigate exactly why medical costs are out of control. Yes, I know, "another commission" but the problem is not with the commissions;

rather, that presidents never utilize their findings. This would be a non-partisan (**no politicians**) commission made up of medical professionals, economists, statisticians, CEOs with proven track records of top flight management, financial planners, experts in fraud investigation, and insurance experts. All of the panel members would have international recognition in their fields.

- Track the care a random number of patients receive during a hospital stay or a visit to the doctor's office and audit TO THE PENNY every procedure no matter how small. Also determine if the procedure or test is necessary.

- Look around the country -- and the world -- for medical facilities and practitioners that are thinking and working outside the box and reducing costs.

- Look at the lowest cost insurance plans available on the market today and study how they work.

- Investigate fraud and then devise procedures to detect and prevent fraud.

- Design a plan that would cover the uninsured through group rates with private insurance carriers paid for (but not managed) by the government. Investigate the model in practice in Switzerland.

- Devise a plan to privatize Medicare while keeping it under government oversight. Implement interstate -- and even international (at least Canada) -- competition and put Medicare policies out for bid. This would make the medical insurance industry much more competitive and offer the buying public many more and cheaper, options. This makes the insurance companies part of the solution instead of part of the problem. Under this concept, the government would only have to oversee these policies and not "manage" every aspect of this program through a huge, costly, and inefficient bureaucracy, as is the case now. This would represent huge savings in medical costs. The states could follow an identical program with Medicaid, which should belong solely to the states.

- Create alternative medical coverage programs that would compete with traditional insurance companies e.g., medical IRAs and medical savings accounts.

- Implement genuine and effective tort reform; frivolous malpractice lawsuits are a big factor in high medical costs.

When this investigation is complete, the President will personally inform the nation of the results in a televised report and detail how the plan is going to be implemented complete with cost analysis and timeframes.

We have been in this mess for decades and we cannot simply drop kick something through the goalposts that will cost hundreds of billions of dollars and create a whole new bureaucracy and a whole new set of problems (Obamacare). It may have to be done incrementally since problems that take decades to develop take time to resolve. By the same token, this study may take years to complete but if that's what it takes to get it right, then so be it.

7. *Dealing With the High Cost of Higher Education*

Education, like medical care, went through the roof when the Government and lending agencies got into the business of financing it. It's another sugar daddy syndrome like the Medical insurance debacle (see above). Phase them out of the picture and replace them with Education IRAs and savings accounts. Education costs are so high because there are lending entities with seemingly unlimited funds willing to loan without questioning the causes behind the costs. Most colleges and universities are old established institutions with strong alumni support. The government could provide scholarships for science and technology AT THE FREE MARKET RATE. Colleges and universities could easily streamline their costs by devoting more time to teaching than research or publishing tomes and tracts that nobody reads. They should scale back on their elaborate building projects and put less emphasis on athletics. Athletics are a major moneymaker but they also add a lot to the costs of running a college and university.

Colleges and universities should dispense with so-called "core curriculums" and focus primarily on the academic major which would reduce the time -- and costs -- of higher education. Graduate degrees focus on the major. Why shouldn't undergraduate degrees? I call this *targeted schooling*.

The interaction provided by the traditional classroom is the ideal but in order to reduce costs, more on line education should be available.

8. *Legislate Controls on Personal Debt*

Personal debt comes from two primary sources: mortgage payments and credit card debt. The Ten Percent Tax would eliminate the mortgage deduction which homebuyers (and sellers) use to justify hyper-inflated housing costs. With that deduction gone, the housing market will become more realistically priced.

(AUTHOR'S NOTE: As of this writing, a lot of people are "under water" meaning their mortgage is more than the current value of their house. This is unfortunate but housing prices need to continue coming down so more people can afford homes.)

Credit card debt could be easily remedied by eliminating pre-approved credit cards and tightening up the application process. Credit cards would be given only to those with a certain credit rating and spending limits would be assigned according to credit rating. Higher spending limits would apply only to those with the best credit. When a cardholder maxes out the spending limit on one card ALL of their credit cards will be automatically suspended. When the cardholder develops a realistic payment plan one -- and only one -- major credit card will be reissued based upon the credit rating of the individual and the new limits may be less than the old but not more. Interest rates on credit cards would also be assigned based on credit rating. Cardholders with poorer credit ratings would be assigned higher interest rates than those with better credit ratings. This would create the specter of a quicker max out if the cards were abused. Credit card interest rates should top out at 15 percent.

All of this being said, credit card companies need to work with customers and develop reasonable and realistic payment plans which would come with the proviso of no more credit card buying until the debt is resolved -- at least to a certain extent.

American credit card debt is $891 billion. We have hit critical mass with this problem and it's time to fix it.

9. *Implement a Gold and Silver Standard*

Right now we are on the paper standard. A Gold and Silver Standard would mandate that the value of our currency is based on the value of our gold and silver reserves. This would increase investor (both foreign and domestic) confidence that our currency is backed up by Precious Metals and not by psychology, emotion, and fear. This would make it more difficult to print money thereby inflating and de-valuing the currency.

10. *Pass a Balanced Budget Amendment*

This would guarantee by law that we could not spend more than we take in. This, together with the implementation of a Precious Metals Standard, would return us to the status of a genuine world economic super power and not one that is living on its past.

11. *Pay off the National Debt*

As of this writing the National Debt is $18 trillion. Possible solutions include debt forgiveness from domestic debtors in return for tax breaks equivalent to money owed. With foreign creditors we could pay down part or all of our debt in goods and services and maybe some good old-fashioned political horse-trading. For example, provide China with free oil at market value (or a little bit less) until they receive oil in the amount equivalent to the money owed them,. While it may sound ambitious, a ten-year plan to accomplish debt liquidation should be our goal. It would be possible if we added debt forgiveness and alternative forms of payment into the mix. It would definitely have to be creative and outside the box but it is doable. One thing is certain -- paying off $18 trillion in the conventional manner is virtually impossible.

Social Security Reform

Everyone talks about Social Security Reform. President George Bush tried to pass some reform legislation in 2005. The cornerstone of that reform legislation which failed was to allow Social Security contributors the ***option*** (operative word) to invest two percent of their contribution as they saw fit. Opponents accused Bush of trying to destroy Social Security. Meanwhile, we are given "drop dead" dates when Social Security will go bankrupt. If I remember correctly, I've heard 2036 and 2042. (Years that could still see me alive. Gulp!!) The government treats this hemorrhaging artery with Band-Aids such as gradually increasing the age when recipients are eligible to receive full benefits. Your year of birth determines when you can draw full benefits.

There are three problems, easily solvable, that are killing Social Security:

(1) It is a government bureaucracy and we all know what government bureaucrats do with money -- spend it, lose it, and waste it.

(2) It has been used as a piggy bank by presidential administrations, at least as far back as Lyndon Johnson, to fund government projects and compensate budget shortfalls.

(3) It is used to supplement welfare (Supplemental Security Income --- SSI) something that was never intended when President Roosevelt signed it into law in 1935. It was originally conceived as an old age retirement fund. Period.

If anyone so much as hints at privatization, the Democrats -- and more than a few Republicans -- go ballistic. But privatization is the only solution. Place the Social Security Administration under private management in the status of a Public Trust under government oversight. Re-name it the National Social Insurance Agency. Employees of the Agency would still be covered by the Federal Employees Retirement System (FERS). Protect it by federal statute from being used as a rainy day fund by the government and separate it from the welfare system.

Under the new Social Security paradigm Social, Security would be a retirement and disability fund only. Employers and employees would still make mandatory contributions; however, Social Security account holders could contribute additional money to their Social Security accounts and receive a more substantial monthly payment, depending upon the amount contributed, when they retire. All contributions, mandatory and voluntary, would be through payroll deduction.   AND, since Social Security would be a private insurance company, it could trade on the New York Stock exchange. A Company that is receiving mandatory payments in the billions every year would be an attractive and lucrative investment.

Some other changes: Social Security account holders would be eligible to draw full benefits at age 65. If an account holder died before retirement, their beneficiaries would be eligible to receive the sum total of their portion of the payments -- mandatory and voluntary -- to the account but not the employer's contribution. A spouse could opt for the decedent's benefits at age 65 if that payment would be higher than the survivor's own monthly benefit amount. In that case the payments would be monthly. All other survivor benefits would be tax free lump sum payments.

The Disability Program would remain in effect.

A privatized National Social Insurance Agency would issue magnetic cards that could be de-activated if lost or stolen as well as a provision for closing out a Social Security account number that was stolen or compromised. New numbers are issued all the time for bank accounts and credit cards so why not for Social Security account numbers? These two policy changes alone would eliminate the overwhelming majority of Social Security fraud and identity theft based on Social Security numbers.

The Government should never have gotten into the insurance business in the first place but it did and there is no turning back. To survive, it needs to be a profit making business not the Ponzi scheme it is today. To be profit making it needs to be given over to the private sector that has the expertise and experience to operate a profit making business.

Immigration Reform

The United States as of this writing is playing host to an estimated thirteen million illegal immigrants and the number is growing every month. Anyone who expresses concern about this is labeled a racist, xenophobe, and anti-immigrant by the dominant Secular Progressive elite. The consequences of this issue get buried in the landfill of phony moralizing, emotion, and political correctness.

Short Term Consequences

An overburdening to the breaking point of the social service infrastructure as illegal immigrants, with the assistance of liberals, Democrats, and businesses employing them, claim as rightful entitlements free education, medical services, and other public assistance benefits available to citizens and legal resident aliens. It's especially easy for illegals to access public services, at least indirectly, if they have a family member who is a U.S. citizen.

An open border for drug gangs, human traffickers, terrorists, and criminal gangs. Mexican drug cartels and organized crime gangs like El Salvador's MS-13 Gang are establishing turf here in the United States. This is creating Black-Brown drug gang wars in cities and prisons not only in the southwest; it is spreading throughout the country.

The current border disaster provides easy access for Al-Qaida and other terrorists to the United States. They simply have to blend in and walk across the border.
In the past couple of years, over one hundred thousand unaccompanied minors from Central America have illegally crossed the border. Many of them were raped, robbed and other wise abused by the "Coyotes" paid to get them here.

The present status quo is creating tensions between the United States and Mexico as Mexico is exporting its poor and unemployed to the United States often with the Mexican Army and Federales running interference for them at the border in clear violation of International Law. There was a time when this would be considered an act of war.

Many of these illegals are dying en route on both sides of the border or indenturing themselves to "Coyotes" who smuggle them across the border for an exorbitant fee.

Long Term Consequences

The eventual Balkanization of the United States: We would become, in Theodore Roosevelt's words, "a polyglot boarding house" and in Pat Buchanan's words, "a nation of squabbling minorities," with a socialist government working full time to appease all of them and accommodate their demands. Whites will be at the bottom of the political food chain as Browns and Blacks use their political clout to demand payback for "stealing" the southwest and slavery. We will become, by 2050, the India of the Western Hemisphere if present trends continue. An Islamic-Fascist Middle East will be the economic and military superpower. Europe is well on its way to becoming Muslim dominated through demographics.
Here is a workable 11 point plan solution:

Secure the border with a high tech fence complete with state-of-the-art surveillance technology augmented with ground and air patrols.

When the border is fully secured, authorize a 3 - 6 month period for illegals to come forward and register. There would be no penalty for them or their employers. Yes, this is *amnesty* but we would have a secure border to support it which we did not have for the Reagan amnesty in the 1980s. And are we really going to deport 13 million people and deal with the problems of constantly looking for them? The expense and the logistics alone make that option nearly impossible.

Implement a "triage" system. Establish criteria to categorize illegals into four groups: **(1)** those eligible for permanent residency; **(2)** Those currently employed and eligible for temporary work visas; **(3)** Those without employment would be deported without prejudice and eligible to return; **(4)** Felons and those with three or more misdemeanors would be deported in persona non grata status.

Illegal immigrants with children and/or spouses who are U.S. citizens or who own property or are otherwise "established" based on government approved criteria would be eligible for Landed Immigrant status. This means they could remain here permanently but with very limited pathways to citizenship: three years of military service or two years in structured public service (e.g., Peace Corps or Americorps).

Other illegal immigrants who are working would be eligible for Guest Worker visas that would be valid for the length of employment and renewable for future employment. Employers would be responsible for notifying the government when a Guest Worker is hired and when they terminate employment. Guest Workers would be able to sponsor their families either at their own or their employer's expense. When the Guest Worker is no longer employed and has no new employment lined up, they would have to leave the country with non-citizen family members.

Illegal immigrants with no employment or scheduled employment would leave the country without prejudice with eligibility for return. This departure would include non-citizen family members.

Illegal immigrants who fail to register during this amnesty period would be deported. If they have one or more felonies or three or more misdemeanors they would be permanently barred from return. Those with no criminal record and who fail to register within the prescribed timeframe would be banned from re-entry for five years. Employers of illegal immigrants who failed to register would be fined $25000.00 per occurrence.

This would be a "clean slate "program." There would be no fines, penalties, or back taxes levied. That would create a bureaucratic quagmire that would cost more to enforce than it would collect.

All future immigrants who illegally enter the country during and after this amnesty period would be deported regardless of circumstances.

American companies could go into Mexico and Central America and recruit directly for jobs that are hard to fill with native born Americans.

All immigrant employment will be captured in an e-verification system. Governments that send students here on government scholarships will
be fined and penalized if their students illegally overstay their visas.
++

We have many illegals who achieved that status by overstaying their visas. Even though these people didn't illegally cross the Rio Grande, they are ultimately in the same status so should be treated the same way.

Immigration is an emotion charged issue. We cannot round up and deport 13 million people both from a logistical and humanitarian point of view. The United States enabled and, dare I say, encouraged illegal immigration through refusal to secure the border and going out of its way to protect illegal immigrants from prosecution and deportation through idiotic policies like "Catch and Release" and Sanctuary Cities. Who can blame impoverished Mexicans and Central Americans from entering the country illegally to take advantage of that? The program I have outlined above is at once both fair and humanitarian and it follows the Rule of Law.

Married Women should keep their Maiden Names

After several decades of Women's Liberation, Western women in general, and American women in particular, for the most part still take their husband's last name; or they hyphenate which is ridiculous and is, in my opinion, a sorry attempt at appeasement (on the husband's part) and political correctness on both sides. If their children marry someone with a hyphenated last name you would have Jason and Tiffany Smith-Jones-Anderson-Brown. The potential for that nonsense to increase exponentially through several generations is chilling. Women in those parts of the world where they are allegedly oppressed do not take their husband's family name. Our tradition has its origins in the Middle Ages when women often came with property or political alliances and the wife was nothing more than a piece of property or a device to further seal an alliance between two families or political entities -- aka a pawn. If modern women had known this in the 1970s, the most fanatical period of the Women's Lib era, they would have pushed for a constitutional amendment to abolish that practice. It would have at least been part of the failed Equal Rights Amendment.

Taking the husband's name in the current culture of divorce and re-marriage generates a host of legal complications and confusion both for the woman and her children. When a woman has a string of last names, it can wreak havoc with Social Security and financial accounts, employment credentials and licenses, or any kind of legal transaction. Theoretically, a woman carries all of her previous husbands' last names e.g., Elizabeth Taylor Hilton-Wilding-Todd-Fisher-Burton-Warner-Burton-Fortensky. (She was married twice to Richard Burton.)

It's time to dump this archaic tradition. It's a holdover from an era that is completely out of context in contemporary reality.